HIGH-OCTANE CAREERS

ER DOCTOR

BY THEIA LAKE

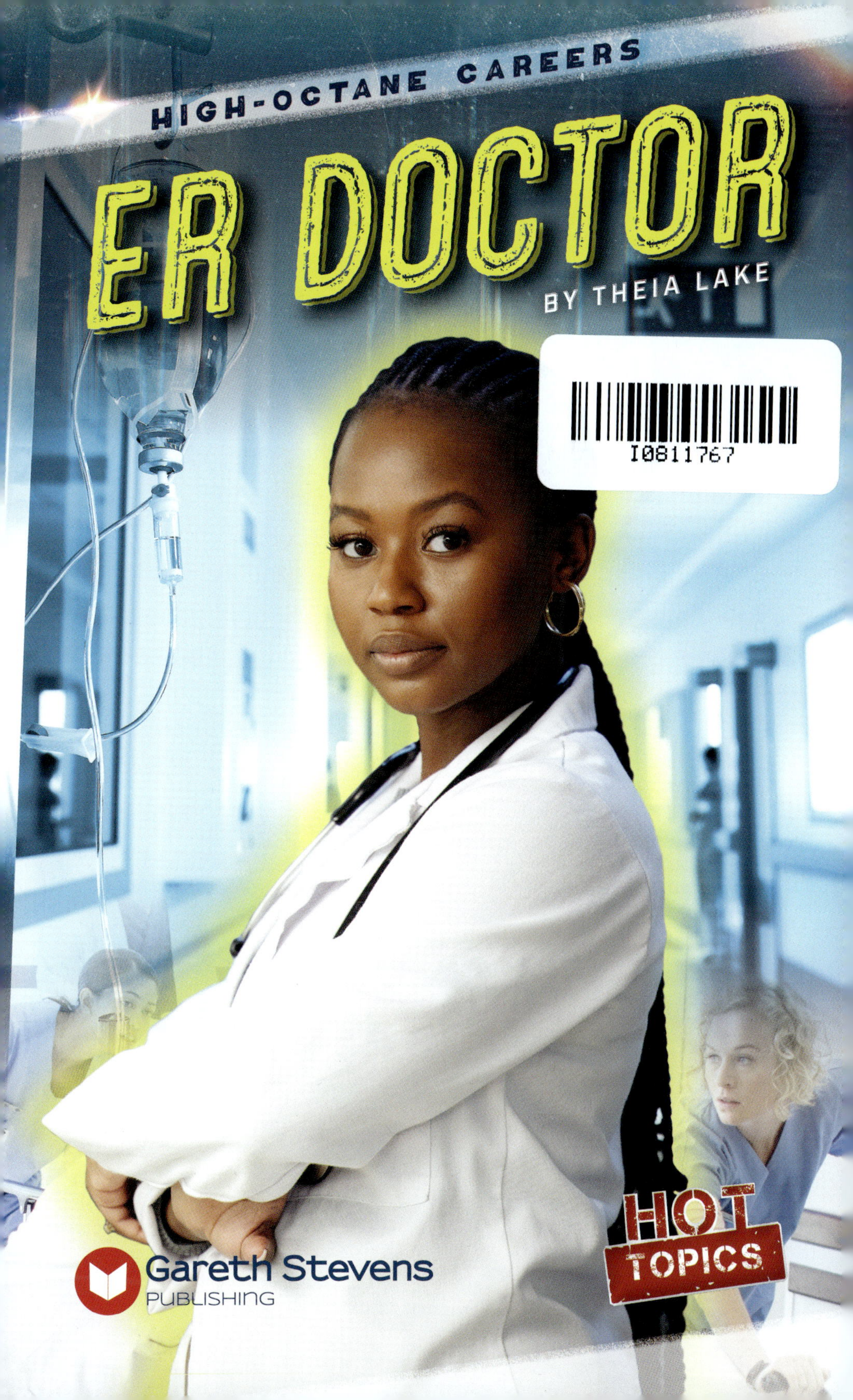

HOT TOPICS

Gareth Stevens PUBLISHING

Please visit our website, www.garethstevens.com. For a free color catalog of all our high-quality books, call toll free 1-800-542-2595 or fax 1-877-542-2596.

Cataloging-in-Publication Data

Names: Lake, Theia.
Title: ER doctor / Theia Lake.
Description: Buffalo, NY : Gareth Stevens Publishing, 2025. | Series: High-octane careers | Includes glossary.
Identifiers: ISBN 9781482469233 (pbk.) | ISBN 9781482469240 (library bound) | ISBN 9781482469257 (ebook)
Subjects: LCSH: Emergency physicians–Juvenile literature. | Emergency medicine–Juvenile literature.
Classification: LCC RA975.5.E5 L25 2025 | DDC 616.02'5'092–dc23

Published in 2025 by
Gareth Stevens Publishing
2544 Clinton Street
Buffalo, NY 14224

Designer: Claire Zimmermann
Editor: Theresa Emminizer

Photo credits: Cover, pp. 1 (man), p. 27 PeopleImages.com - Yuri A/Shutterstock.com; cover, p.1 (hospital background) sfam_photo/Shutterstock.com; cover, p. 1 (lower photo) KOTOIMAGES/Shutterstock.com; cover, p.1 (series title light flare) SpicyTruffel/Shutterstock.com; series art (background texture) Golubovy/Shutterstock.com; p. 4 Dolores M. Harvey/Shutterstock.com; pp. 5, 29 Monkey Business Images/Shutterstock.com; p. 7 H_Ko/Shutterstock.com; p. 9 Nuttapong punna/Shutterstock.com; p. 11 RONNACHAIPARK/Shutterstock.com; p. 13 Frame Stock Footage/Shutterstock.com; p. 15 totojang1977/Shutterstock.com; p. 17 Rey Light Perspectives/Shutterstock.com; p. 19 FOTO Eak/Shutterstock.com; p. 21 ARLOU_ANDREI/Shutterstock.com; p. 23 Supavadee butradee/Shutterstock.com; p. 25 Krakenimages.com/Shutterstock.com; p. 30 (icons) AP Stock/Shutterstock.com.

Some of the images in this book illustrate individuals who are models. The depictions do not imply actual situations or events.

Printed in the United States of America

CPSIA compliance information: Batch #CWGS25: For further information contact Gareth Stevens, at 1-800-542-2595.

CONTENTS

SAVING LIVES

When someone gets hurt, who's there to help? ER doctors are! ER doctors do lifesaving work at all hours of the day and night. They take care of people who are **dangerously** sick or hurt. ER doctors are quick-thinking, fast-acting heroes!

UNDER PRESSURE!

ER is short for Emergency Room. An emergency is an unexpected **situation** that needs quick action. An ER is the part of the hospital where emergency medical problems are treated.

ASSESSING THE PATIENT

When a patient comes into the ER, the first thing the doctor does is **assess** their condition, or state. The doctor looks at the patient's body, finds out about their medical history, and orders tests to learn more about the problem.

UNDER PRESSURE!

Patients are triaged based on the doctor's assessment. Triage is a way of sorting patients based on the **severity** of their problem and the kind of care they need.

DIAGNOSING THE PROBLEM

Based on the assessment, doctors then diagnose the patient. Diagnosing means identifying, or figuring out and naming, what the patient's problem is. In an emergency room, all of this is done very quickly. Sometimes ER doctors must make decisions within minutes!

UNDER PRESSURE!

Diagnosing medical conditions isn't easy. Doctors must closely observe, or look at, a patient's symptoms. Symptoms are signs that something's wrong with your body.

EMERGENCY TREATMENT

Some patients that come to the ER have life-threatening, or deadly, conditions. They need treatment immediately (right away) to stabilize their body, or bring it back under control. If someone's heart stops, ER doctors try to resuscitate them. Resuscitation is bringing someone back to life.

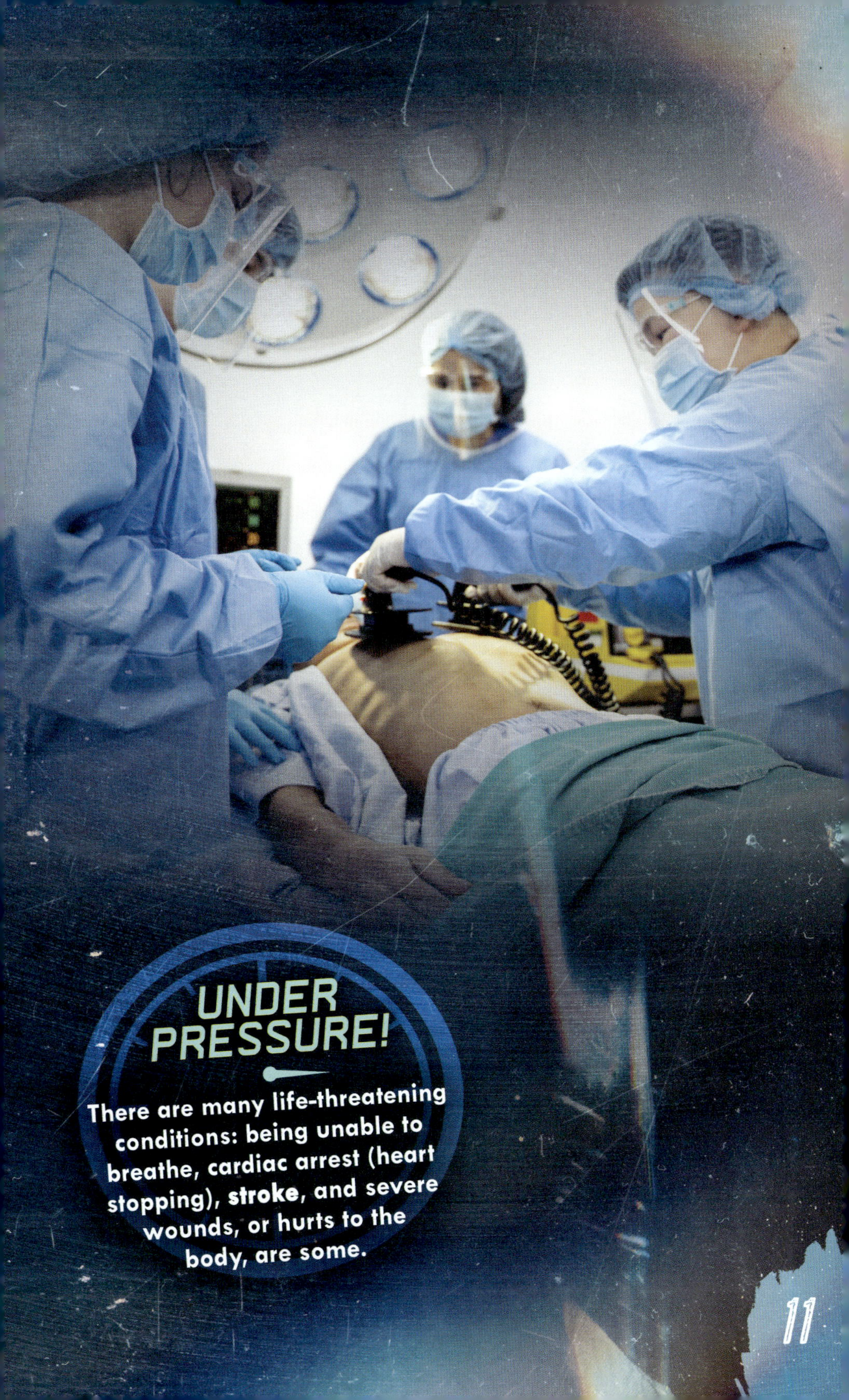

UNDER PRESSURE!

There are many life-threatening conditions: being unable to breathe, cardiac arrest (heart stopping), **stroke**, and severe wounds, or hurts to the body, are some.

COORDINATING CARE

After assessing, diagnosing, and stabilizing the patient, ER doctors coordinate, or plan, how they'll be cared for. Patients may need more tests. They may be transferred, or moved, to another part of the hospital where they can be treated by a specialist.

UNDER PRESSURE!

ER doctors don't usually perform **surgeries**. They can do some minor (small) surgical procedures, but usually transfer patients for more serious surgeries.

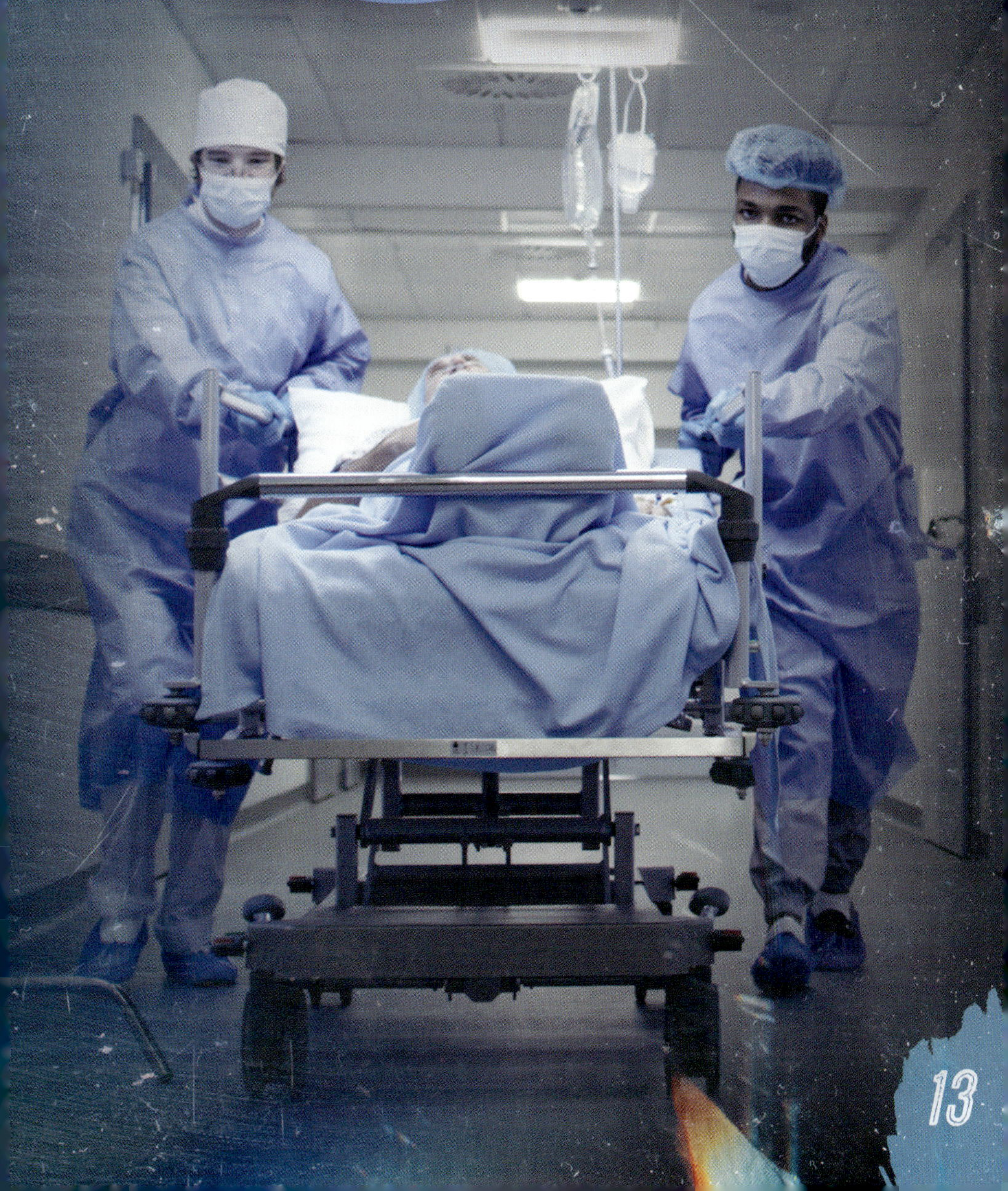

DISCHARGING THE PATIENT

When a patient is discharged, or let out, from the ER, the ER doctor gives them directions about what they should do next. ER doctors write careful records about what happened to the patient and what kind of care they were given.

UNDER PRESSURE!

After a visit to the ER, patients usually follow up with their primary care physician (PCP). PCPs are regular doctors who patients see for yearly checkups and non-emergency issues.

KINDS OF ER DOCTORS

ER doctors must be able to treat many different kinds of illnesses and injuries. But some ER doctors specialize in certain types of medical care. For example, Pediatric Emergency Physicians care for babies and children. Toxicologists specialize in treating people who have been poisoned.

UNDER PRESSURE!

Disaster medicine specialists treat people in disasters, or large emergencies. They are the first helpers on the scene when many people get sick or are hurt.

PRE-MED EDUCATION

How does someone become an ER doctor? First, they must earn a bachelor's (four-year) **degree**. A pre-med program in college helps students prepare for medical school. Then, they must pass the Medical College Admission Test (MCAT) to continue on to medical school.

UNDER PRESSURE!

While completing their bachelor's degree, pre-med students usually study science subjects, such as biology, which is the study of living things.

MEDICAL SCHOOL

Medical school programs take about four years to complete. During the first two years, students learn in the classroom and laboratory (a place with tools to perform experiments). The second two years are spent in hospitals gaining hands-on **experience** under the leadership of real doctors.

UNDER PRESSURE!

Training in a real hospital helps students decide what kind of medicine is a good fit for them. ER doctoring is a difficult path.

MEDICAL RESIDENCY

After completing medical school, it's time to begin a medical residency program. This is another period of hands-on training, overseen by a doctor. Residents work full time, usually 60 to 80 hours a week. Residency programs last from three to seven years.

UNDER PRESSURE!

Some people also decide to do a medical fellowship. Fellowships are one or two years of training in a particular kind of doctoring, such as pediatric emergency medicine.

LICENSURE

Each state has its own set of rules about how a doctor can become licensed. However, most require passing the United States Medical Licensing Examination (USMLE). ER doctors may need special certification from the American Board of Emergency Medicine (ABEM).

UNDER PRESSURE!

A license is a piece of paper that allows someone to do something. A certification states that someone has been trained and educated to do something.

SPECIAL SKILLS

ER doctors must be good at multitasking, or doing many things at once. They never know how many patients, or what kinds of wounds or illnesses they're going to see in a day! ER doctors must have strong nerves to deal with scary situations and stay calm no matter what.

UNDER PRESSURE!

ER doctors need to be able to work well with others. They must **communicate** facts and directions with teammates and patients.

DO YOU HAVE WHAT IT TAKES?

Does being an ER doctor sound exciting to you? The path is long and hard, but it's well worth the work. ER doctors are true heroes. They work long hours, all day and night, making choices and giving treatments that save people's lives.

UNDER PRESSURE!

Being an ER doctor is a very stressful job. It's important for doctors to take care of their health and well-being.

U.S. EMERGENCY ROOM FAST FACTS

About 139.8 MILLION people visit the ER each year.

ER VISIT RATES ARE HIGHEST for babies under one year old and adults 75 years and over.

About 40 PERCENT of patients are seen in fewer than 15 MINUTES.

About 40 MILLION people are seen in the ER for injuries (including poisoning).

About 18 MILLION people are admitted to the hospital after visiting the ER.

FOR MORE INFORMATION

BOOKS

Bolte, Mari. *Important Jobs at Hospitals.* North Mankato, MN: Spark, an imprint of Capstone, 2023.

Miller, Marie-Therese. *Jobs in Health Care.* Minneapolis, MN: Core Library, an imprint of Abdo Publishing, 2024.

WEBSITES

Kids Health
kidshealth.org/en/kids/emergency.html
Read these helpful tips about what to do in an emergency and when to call 911.

Kids Konnect
kidskonnect.com/careers/doctor/#Kinds_of_Doctors
Find out more about the different types of doctors and what they do.

Publisher's note to educators and parents: Our editors have carefully reviewed these websites to ensure that they are suitable for students. Many websites change frequently, however, and we cannot guarantee that a site's future contents will continue to meet our high standards of quality and educational value. Be advised that students should be closely supervised whenever they access the internet.

GLOSSARY

assess: To make a judgment about something.

dangerously: Very unsafe.

communicate: To share thoughts or feelings by sound, movement, or writing.

degree: An official paper given to someone who has completed certain classes at a college or university.

experience: Skills gained by doing something.

severity: How severe, or very bad and serious, something is.

situation: A set of conditions or circumstances.

stroke: A sudden blockage or break of a blood vessel in the brain.

surgery: A medical treatment used for injuries and illnesses that involves operations.

INDEX